My Village

Translated by C.J. Moore

Original works by Hansi are at the Hansi Museum,
Musée Hansi in Riquewihr, near Colmar, France

First published in France in 1913 by Editions Floury, Paris
As *Mon Village – Ceux qui n'oublient pas*
First (slightly abridged) English edition published in 2008 by Floris Books
Edinburgh together with La Nuée Bleue / DNA, Strasbourg

© La Nuée Bleue / DNA, Strasbourg www.nueebleue.com
English version © 2008 Floris Books, Edinburgh www.florisbooks.co.uk

British Library CIP data available
ISBN 978-086315-656-4 (Floris Books)
ISBN 978-2-7165-0596-3 (La Nuée Bleue)

Printed in Poland

My Village

HANSI

Floris Books

At the time that this book was published in 1913, Alsace had been annexed by Germany for forty years following the Franco-Prussian war of 1870–71. Despite its dialect having a German origin — which is still spoken by some of its people today — Alsace was a French region with profoundly republican values.

The village I'm going to describe isn't made up: it really exists. To find it, you have to travel deep into the countryside of Alsace in France. Get off the train at a small station decorated with flowers, and walk down a narrow road between some orchards. In the distance you'll see the church spire rising above the wheat fields. If you arrive on a Sunday, you'll see the villagers coming out of church: the young girls in their traditional black bonnets, young men wearing black and red and older folk who still wear a wide frock coat and three-pointed hat.

Of course, the outfits in my pictures are not worn these days. War came to Alsace and our land was occupied by the Germans. Many of our traditions disappeared forever. New industry and the railways brought horrible cheap German clothes and other items to my village. The local policemen are German too and they have brought many unpopular and interfering new laws.

This pretty village is no longer officially part of France. But the young children still play at being French soldiers, and the older folk are proud of their role in the war. The heart and soul of Alsace remains strong.

1913   *Hansi*

There is a little village in Alsace which is tucked away among gentle hills, surrounded by fields of flowers and orchards. Above the houses is a huge grassy slope dotted with daisies and forget-me-nots. This is where the children play.

Just like everywhere, the boys catch beetles and make them do tricks on a piece of string. Or they play at being soldiers, fighting the policeman's children. The girls dance round in circles and gather bunches of flowers. Their red or blue skirts look a bit like flowers too. Hand in hand they go, singing ancient songs which take on a new meaning.

The main road leads to a hilltop from where you can see Strasbourg cathedral, or you can follow a track between the hawthorn bushes to the little cemetery on the edge of the wood. Here are the simple graves of soldiers who died in the great battle forty years ago.

On a spring evening, looking out over the village with its smoking chimneys, the church tower, the central square where the liberty tree still grows, the schoolhouse with a storks' nest on the roof, young people walking hand in hand and old folk chatting on their doorsteps, when the birds and children are singing, you'd think this would be the happiest village on earth.

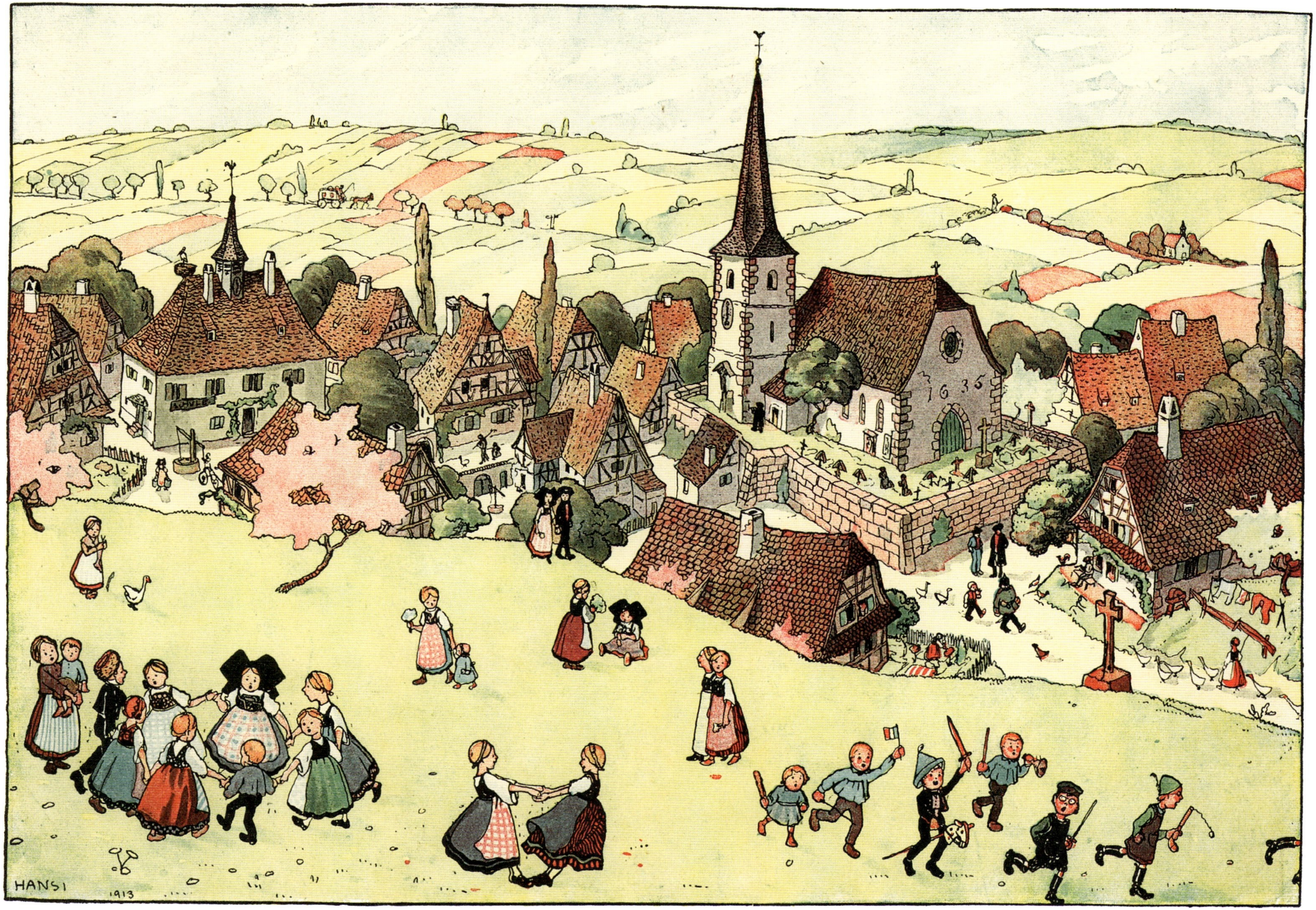
1635
HANSI
1913

The children love it when the storks arrive back. First to appear is old Grandmother Stork. She glides over the houses and perches briefly on the schoolhouse roof, before flying back to let the other storks know the nest is still there and the children are waiting.

You might think at first glance that the storks come from Germany: their wings are black and white — the colours of Prussia — their beak is also very big, and when they cannot find enough food in the north they go off to other countries. But our little children are not so easily fooled by appearances, and there is a deep love for the storks.

At last, the waiting is over and Mother Stork flies straight to the nest while Father Stork swoops over the rooftops. The children run out, shouting and cheering, because now they know spring is not far away. Suddenly, it all goes quiet: the children hold hands in a huge circle and sing the ancient song to welcome the storks while the schoolteacher keeps time. Mother Stork, high up on the nest, seems pleased: she ruffles her feathers and looks thoughtful.

Stork, stork, you are lucky. You've spent all your years in France. Stork, stork, in your beak bring a lit-tle French sol-dier.

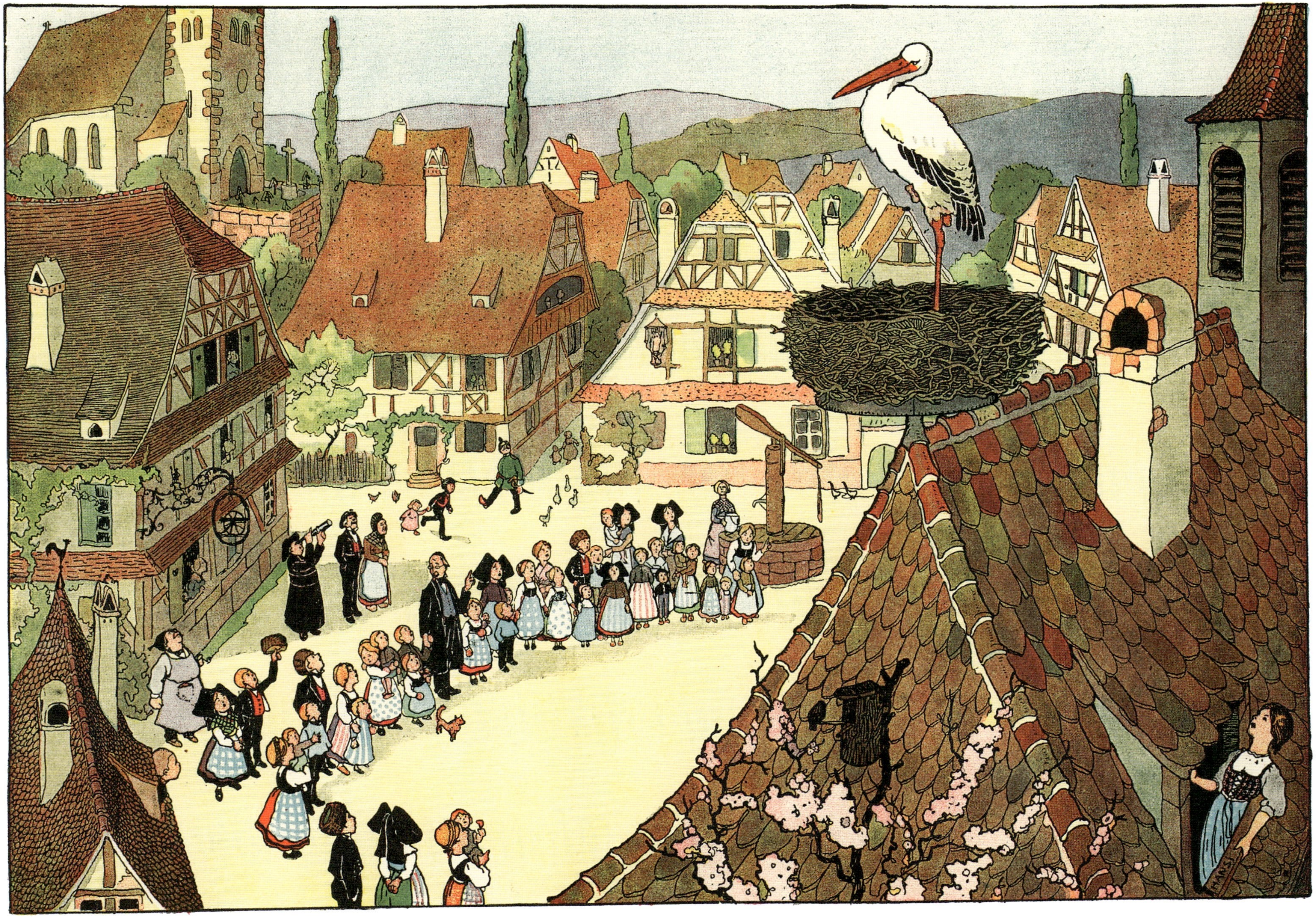

There are two schoolteachers in the village. Father Vetter is very old and everyone loves him. Before the war he taught French and even now, when a child goes to France, Father Vetter teaches them the words they need to know and helps them enjoy speaking French.

Nothing is better than when he tells of the terrible battles of the last war, when the schoolhouse became an army hospital and the streets were littered with discarded armour while the German armies marched through. The little girls cry, and the eyes of the boys shine as they dream of an end to these injustices. Father Vetter wears an old-fashioned frock coat, like many of the older folk in the village. He looks at you kindly over a pair of spectacles that bounce on his nose. He is always invited to weddings and family occasions, and the children never play tricks on him.

One day, the government decided he was too old for the job, and sent a young German teacher to be his assistant. The new teacher is not very friendly. He wears a green cloth jacket and speaks in very formal German. He works for a German newspaper in Strasbourg.

He always carries a cane which he uses to beat the schoolchildren — all, that is, except the policeman's children. He thinks he knows everything, but in his lessons the children only learn to recite patriotic German songs by heart. In spite of the cane, the children play more tricks on him in a single week than they did on Father Vetter in his whole career.

7

Most of the children love Sunday. To begin with, they can lie in — but only if they've polished their shoes the night before. When they get up, they have to dress smartly. The mothers do the girls' hair, bunching it in neat coils around their ears, and dress them in pretty patterned skirts, embroidered bodices and their best Sunday bonnets. The boys wash their cheeks so hard they glow, then get dressed like their fathers in black suits with a red waistcoat — the same red as a French soldier's trousers. When the church bell rings, off they all go.

Sadly, not all the village children are happy. There is a little boy called Georges Klipfel, known as Yerri, who has had a hard life. Yerri lived with his mother and father in a pretty house with a lovely garden. Then, on the fourteenth of July, his father celebrated a patriotic French holiday which was banned by the Germans. He also said some disrespectful things about His Majesty, the King of Prussia, which is a terrible crime.

A passing German musician overheard him and ran to tell the policeman. Yerri's father quickly left for France so that he wouldn't be sent to jail. But the Germans took Yerri's house and garden, and sold them. Yerri's mother was so upset she soon died. Yerri now lives with his grandfather.

Yerri's father joined the French Foreign Legion and fought bravely in Africa. Soon, he will be able to leave the army and get a job in France. Yerri and his grandfather will probably go and live with him there, and we won't see them around the village any more.

9

Yerri loves his grandfather very much. Here they are on their way to church. In his hymn book, Yerri keeps some pictures and a ribbon sent to him from France by his father.

Many homes have similar tales of hardship. But you'd never know, because the people of Alsace don't complain. Surely the terrible brutalities they have suffered cannot last for ever.

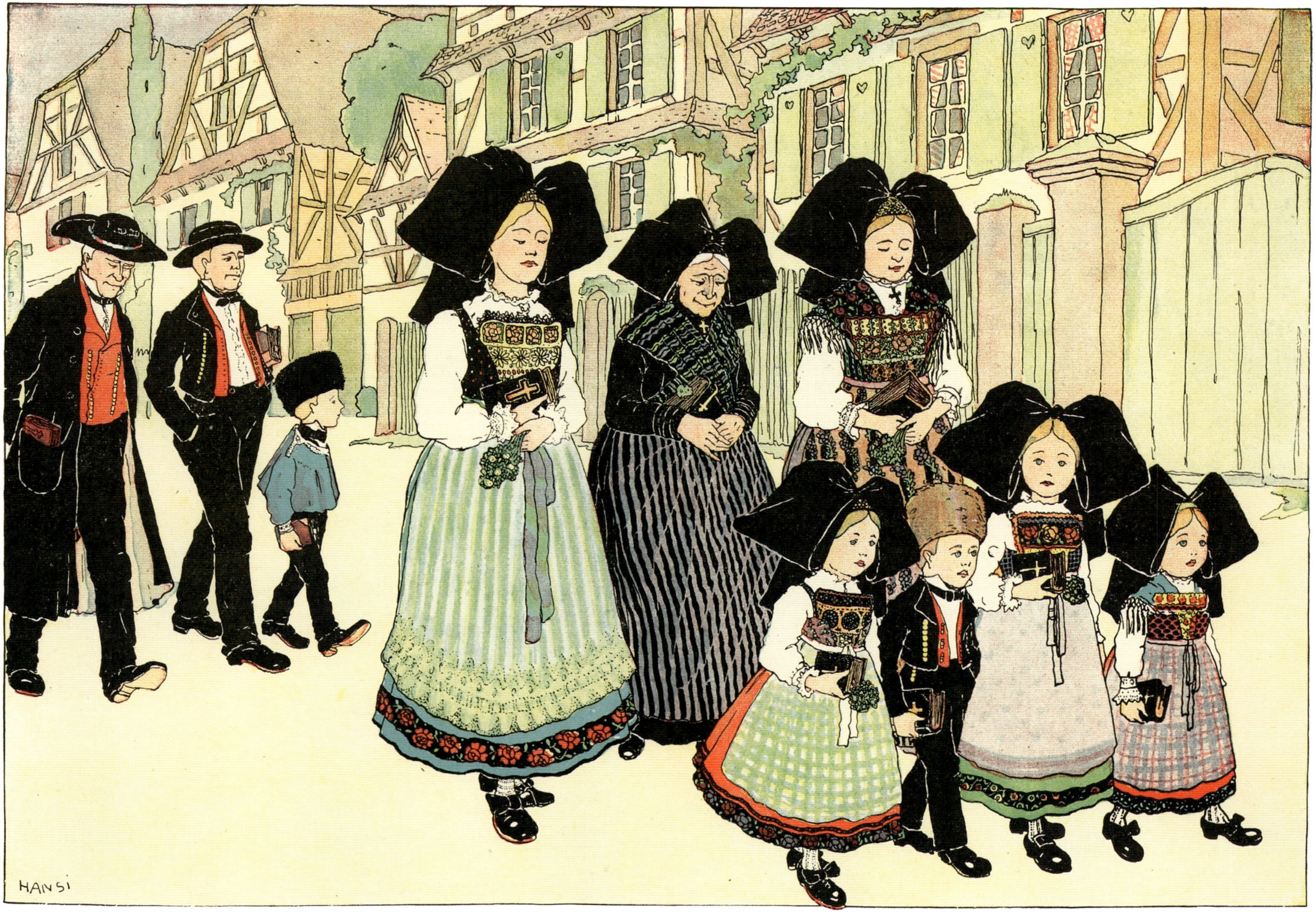
HANSI

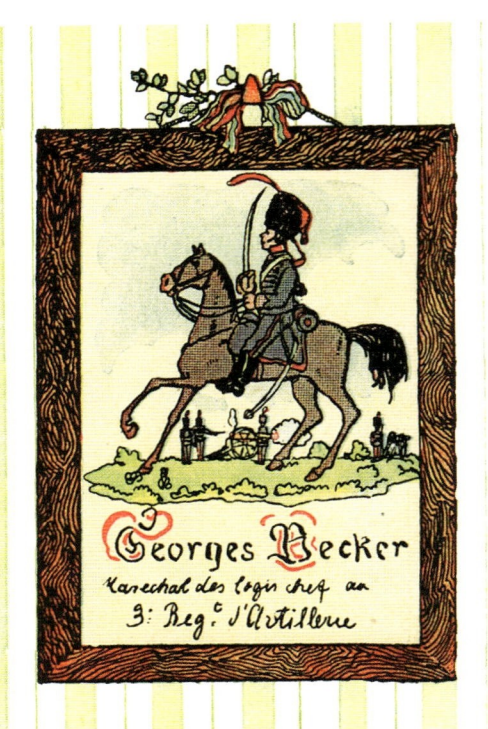

Here, coming down the street, are three men from a time gone by. They are all veterans of the old French army. The oldest, a tall man called Schimmel, was a cavalryman. At home he has a portrait of himself in uniform, sitting on his horse. He rode into battle at Morsbronn, just nearby, and must have been a frightening sight. Every Sunday, he strides from his doorway to join his old friends, Georges Becker, who was a mounted gunner, and Martin Spohr, who was an elite light infantry soldier.

The three of them walk down the street in their frock coats, their medals glinting in the sunshine. They don't speak very much — some say that others speak too much. In fact, the village street is very quiet, because my village likes silence more than voices of anger. Through the sound of the footsteps and the chimes of the bells however, I can hear the vow made by our fathers: *We swear, for ourselves, our children and their descendants, to stand up for the eternal right of the people of Alsace and Lorraine to belong to the French nation.*

13

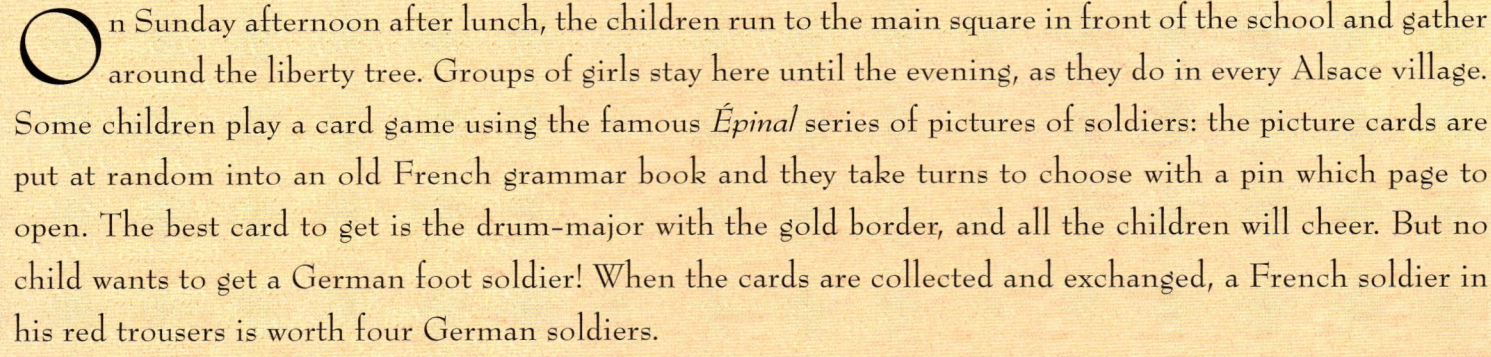

On Sunday afternoon after lunch, the children run to the main square in front of the school and gather around the liberty tree. Groups of girls stay here until the evening, as they do in every Alsace village. Some children play a card game using the famous *Épinal* series of pictures of soldiers: the picture cards are put at random into an old French grammar book and they take turns to choose with a pin which page to open. The best card to get is the drum-major with the gold border, and all the children will cheer. But no child wants to get a German foot soldier! When the cards are collected and exchanged, a French soldier in his red trousers is worth four German soldiers.

Now across the square comes the policeman's family. The policeman himself leads the way with his wife, and his daughters and sons — Irmentrude, Hildegarde, Elsa and Hilda, Wilhelm, Siegfried, Karlchen and Hanschen — follow on behind. They arrive at the liberty tree, and the birds stop singing.

15

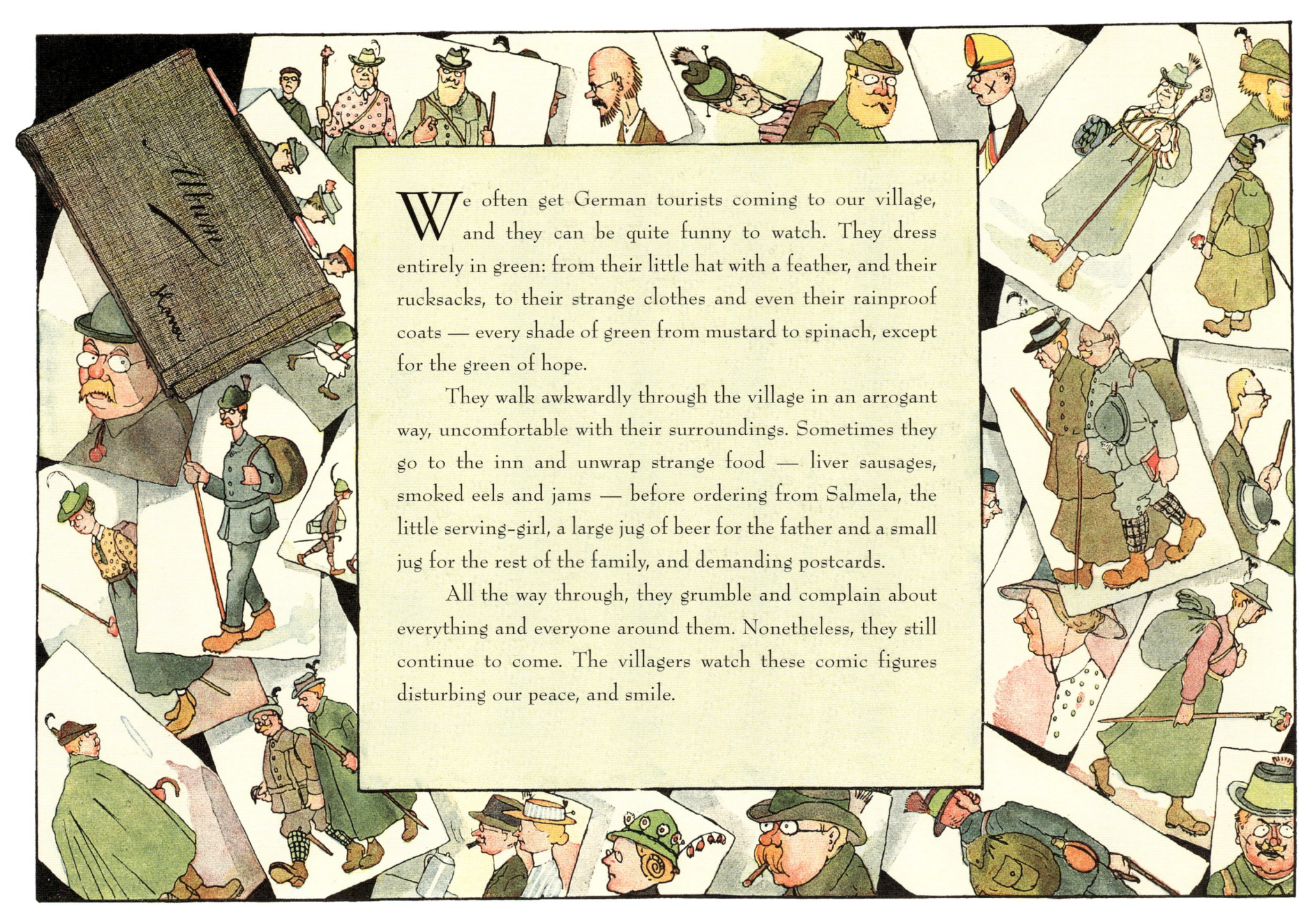

We often get German tourists coming to our village, and they can be quite funny to watch. They dress entirely in green: from their little hat with a feather, and their rucksacks, to their strange clothes and even their rainproof coats — every shade of green from mustard to spinach, except for the green of hope.

They walk awkwardly through the village in an arrogant way, uncomfortable with their surroundings. Sometimes they go to the inn and unwrap strange food — liver sausages, smoked eels and jams — before ordering from Salmela, the little serving-girl, a large jug of beer for the father and a small jug for the rest of the family, and demanding postcards.

All the way through, they grumble and complain about everything and everyone around them. Nonetheless, they still continue to come. The villagers watch these comic figures disturbing our peace, and smile.

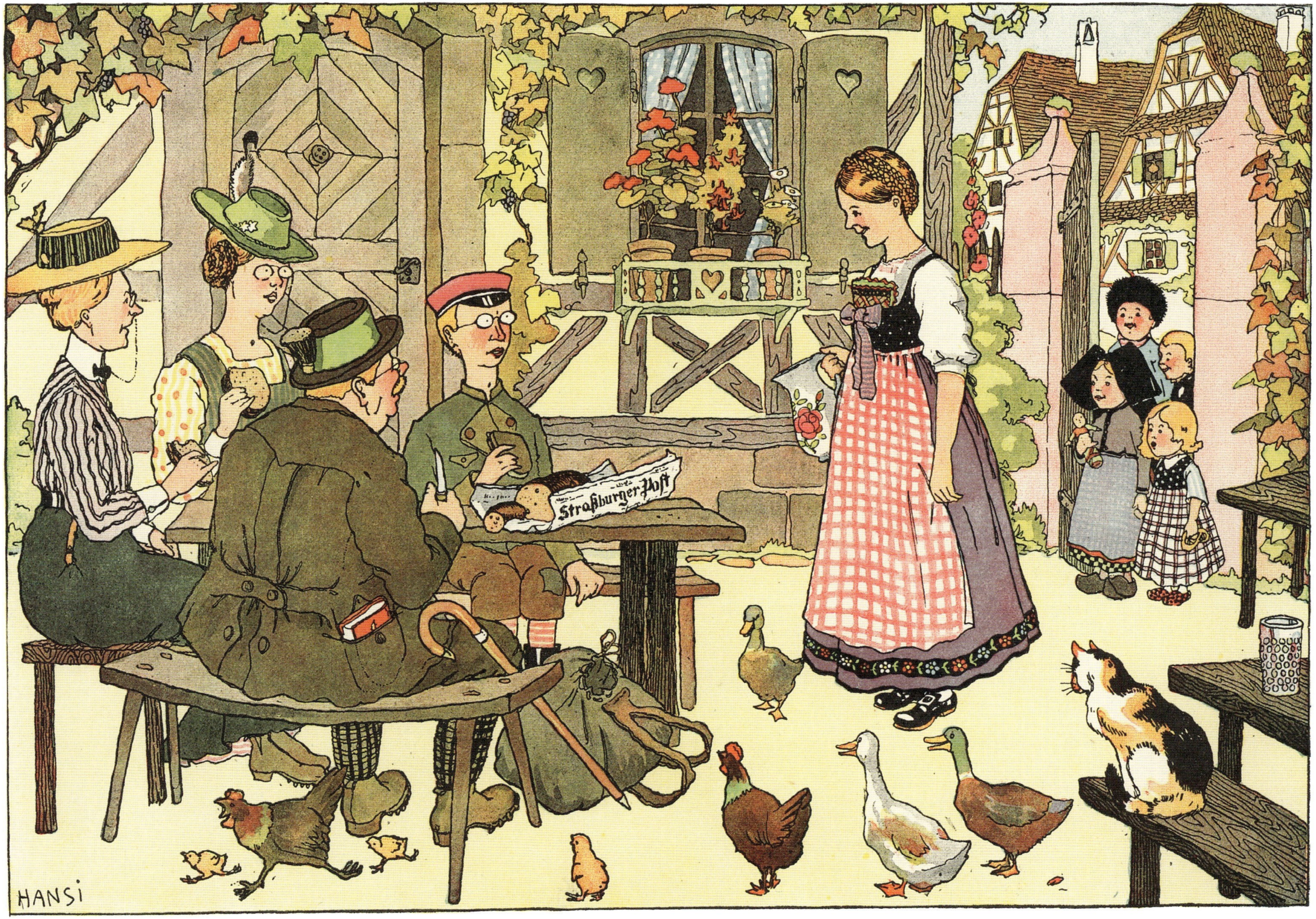
Straßburger Post
HANSI

Sometimes we get French tourists, which everyone enjoys. They arrive in a handsome car, usually with a helpful man who explains everything about traditional Alsace clothes. The women are always pretty, wearing lovely veils and beautiful little hats, and even the children are pleasant. Yes, the French visitors always think our village is pretty. You would think that, although they're from Paris where they have everything, they've never seen a stork before, because they love seeing ours so much.

The French children quickly make friends with our little ones. Their mother hands out sweets wrapped in silver and gold, a kind we never see in our village. Then our French friends take photographs, we say goodbye and, in particular, "see you again!" and we watch with envy as they drive off towards the land of freedom.

19

Every autumn, after the storks have gone, we celebrate the annual village festival, called the *Messti*. On the evening before, every house is filled with the smells of baking. Mother musn't be disturbed because she's busy cooking, mysteriously producing wonderful plum and apple tarts, and a huge *Kougelhopf,* our traditional fruit bread. When she's done, if the children have been good, she lets them come into the kitchen and use up the rest of the dough making Alsatian *Bretzels*, large crispy salt breads with a soft centre.

In the evening, the bigger children carefully carry huge tarts — with fruit slices neatly lined up and topped with strips of golden pastry — through the village to the baker's oven for cooking. The little children follow on behind, keeping the chickens and geese away.

They pass in front of Karlchen, one of the policeman's sons, who is chewing on his piece of black bread and watching them jealously. Why is it, he thinks, that he, the son of a conquering hero, is eating a bit of hard crust, while these *Wackes,* as his father calls them (a rude German word for people from Alsace), parade delicious cakes right before his eyes?

21

Like all Alsatian festivals, the *Messti* begins with an enormous family meal: soup with dumplings, stewed hare with noodles, then a big roast. Friends and family from nearby villages arrive in time for pudding, carrying their baskets and umbrellas.

Officially, the feast can't start until the policeman has done his rounds. He has to make sure the German flag is raised higher than all others. Then he checks the cake stall to make sure there are no pastries wrapped in red, white and blue. This will sound ridiculous, but apparently the German Empire, with its thousands of soldiers, fortresses, guns, armour and Zeppelins, will be in great danger if, during our festival, a boy were to blow a tune through a paper roll made of French colours!

But everything is in order. The festival can begin, and here come the musicians leading the way. The prettiest girl in the village presents the mayor with a cake of honour, and then it's time for the dance which lasts until the early hours of the morning. Eventually the last guests go home, carrying big slices of fruit bread wrapped in napkins.

Vve SILBEREISEN
AU GRAND St NICOLAS
COMPAGNIE FRANÇAISE CHOCOLAT SCHAAL
PAINS D'ÉPICES DE GERTWILLER
HANSI

There's another festival that some would like us to celebrate with as much enthusiasm as we do the *Messti:* the feast-day of the Emperor, in January. The German schoolteacher organizes a ceremony with a patriotic song and a boring speech, but only the policeman's children join in the final three cheers. Our children open their mouths and pretend to sing, but no sound comes out — just like I did at their age.

But a day's holiday is always welcome, and the children often go to a nearby town to watch their celebrations. The Germans put on fancy dress: the little boys wear pointed helmets and brandish swords, and the girls wear cross-ribbons in German colours. Fat councillors and teachers squeeze into their old military uniforms, and those without a uniform pin a handful of medals to their chest — medals of as many different classes as you'll find on a train, including a bright yellow ribbon given to every soldier alive in 1897, for some centenary or other.

The best sight is around five o'clock: the invited guests stagger out of the big official banquet, and because it's often quite icy, these worthy councillors, business leaders, teachers and accountants can barely stay on their feet. Then the inns fill up and you can hear their croaking cheers like birds of prey, deep into the winter night.

When I was little, I always thought that on a day like this, the French would have no trouble at all re-taking Alsace.

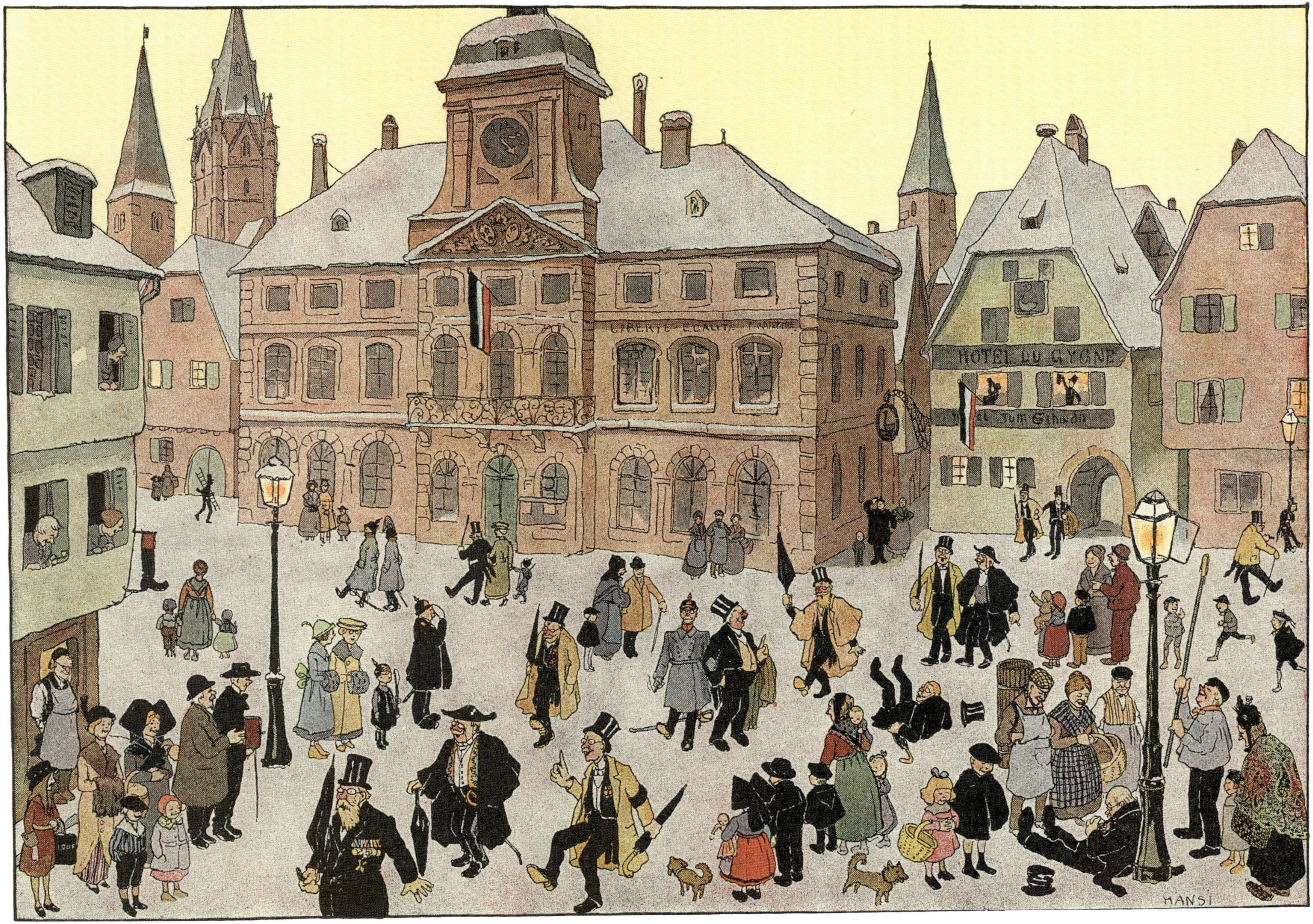
LIBERTE EGALITE
HOTEL DU CYGNE
HANSI

After all that eating and drinking, we often feel the need to reconnect with the true spirit of our land. For that, there's no better place than the battle sites of our nation. I don't mean rows of marble and bronze sculptures, where you're as likely to meet some German veterans noisily celebrating some anniversary or other. No, we go to places where simple stone pillars and small crosses mark the sites where French soldiers fought to the end, where local children leave bunches of wild flowers.

When we visit a French monument which remembers three occasions where our people battled against the invader, looking out across the evening landscape, our hearts fill with deep emotion. The proud bronze cockerel seems to come to life, and the ranks of our gallant soldiers gather to answer its cry.

That is a celebration of the heart that no government can take from us.

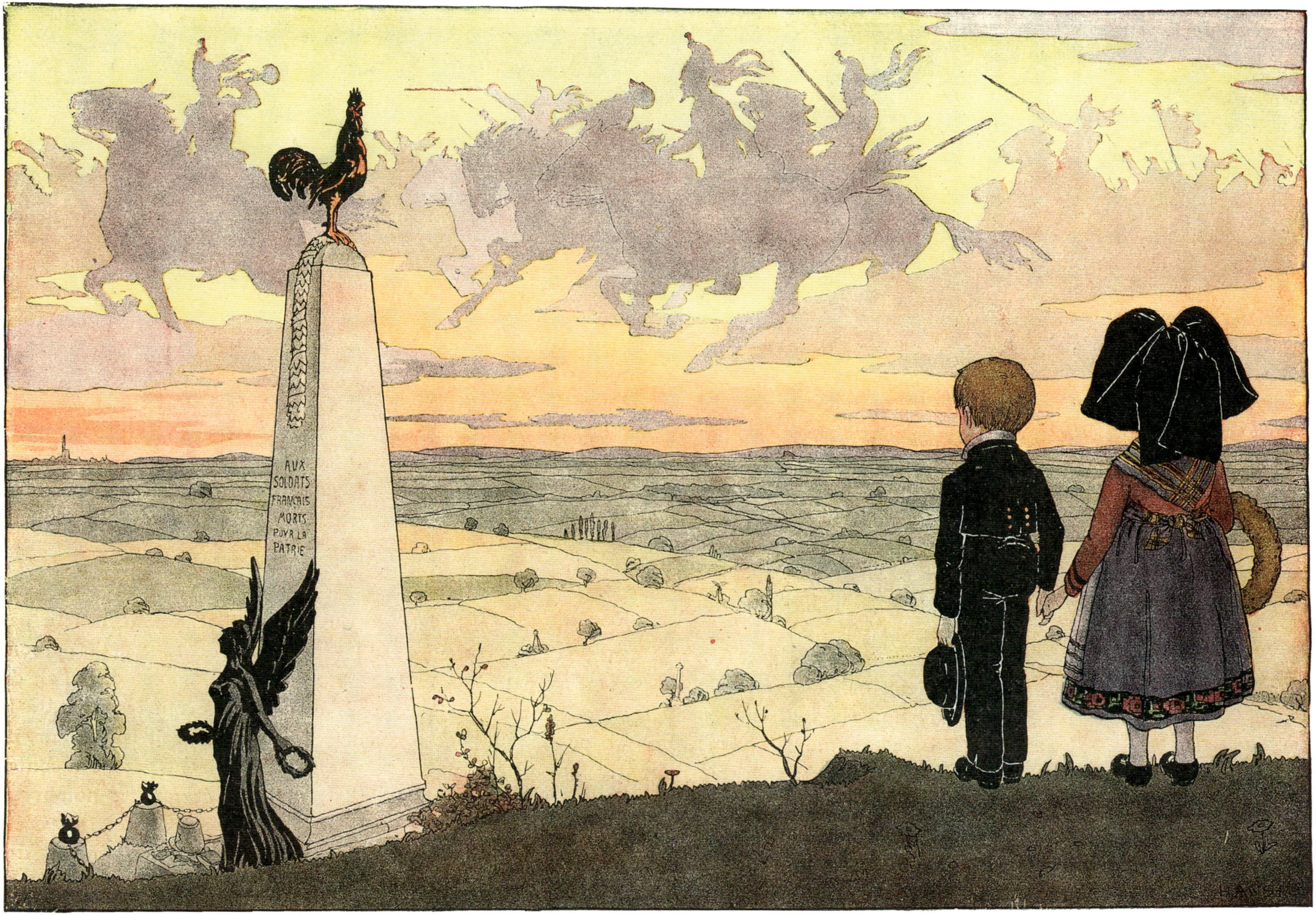
AUX
SOLDATS
FRANÇAIS
MORTS
POUR LA
PATRIE

The best feast-day of all, of course, the fourteenth of July, cannot be celebrated in our village. Every child dreams of going to Nancy, across the border, to see the parade. Those who are lucky enough to go set off early in the morning, laughing all the way, and arrive back late at night, their wagon decorated with garlands.

It's a long tiring day, but while in Nancy, they're able to cry out the sorrow that weighed them down, and store up enough joy to last them through the coming months.

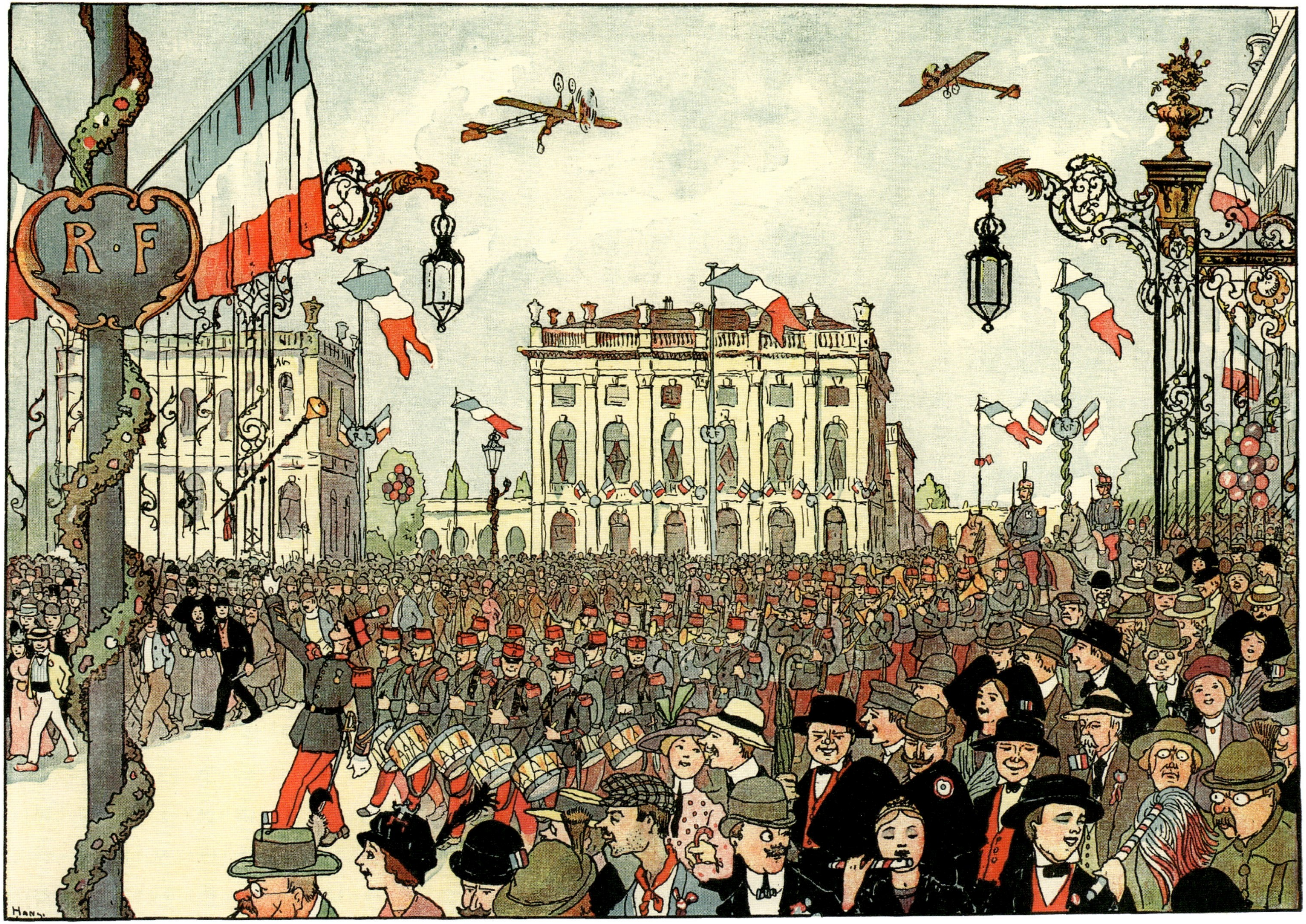
R·F

Before we reach the end, I want to introduce you to another village friend: Old Spinner, the nightwatchman. He was a gunner in the old French army and he still wears his military coat when he does his rounds (French cloth never wears out!). In one hand he carries a long axe with a spike, known as a *halberd,* and in the other he carries a lantern. A horn is slung across his chest, ready to sound the alarm. All night long he walks the village streets, wishing good things for those asleep in their beds.

Old Spinner has been spending more time in the local inn recently, because every time he hears that a Zeppelin has had a big accident, where no one was hurt, he goes to buy a half litre of wine. In the inn, he tells great tales about his army days in the Crimea, Mexico and Italy.

The other day, some younger men were teasing him, asking how such a valiant soldier could have been beaten by the Germans. He shrugged and said, "Well yes, we were beaten. But that's because we let them win! That way, we can have the pleasure of beating the Prussians the next time. The colonel himself told me that." Not one of the younger men laughed, because they all felt the power of the old man's faith in his country.

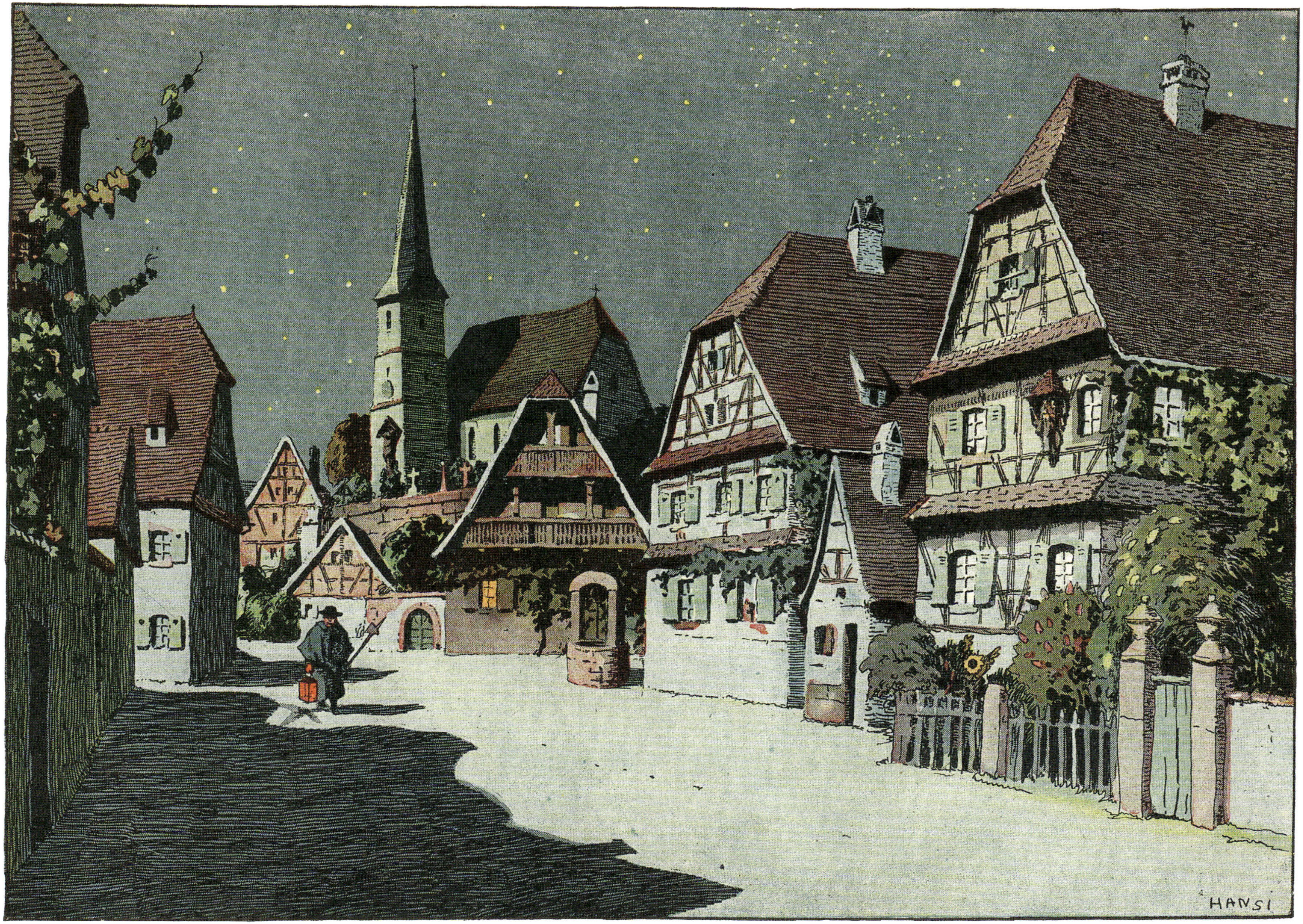
HANSI

Indeed, when I see our poor people weighed down by taxes, overwhelmed by German immigration, or insulted by some stuffed-up parade-ground soldier, when I feel despair and decide that life in Alsace is just too sad, at such moments the wonderful stubbornness of that old soldier comes to mind. Then I, too, hope against hope that better days will come and fine people like him will be treated fairly, and my village will be full of free and happy people.

My village is asleep now. The younger children have been in bed some time already, perhaps dreaming about Christmas or the parade in Nancy. The dark silhouette of the church tower stands out against the starry sky. The old battlefield, with the white tombstones of heroes, stretches across the distant countryside.

The main village street is quiet. No more shrill patriotic tunes come from the policeman's house. A dog barks; another, further away, replies. In the little gardens, fireflies hover and pretend to be stars.

A light appears around the corner, and the nightwatchman's voice calls slowly. At Father Vetter's house, a few locals have gathered to hear him translate the latest news from forbidden French newspapers brought back from Nancy. He talks about the French army, of aeroplanes and those who fly them, of people in faraway places who have at last thrown off their invaders. And now, in the darkness, his is the only light left shining in my village.

EPILOGUE

From the Epilogue

One sultry day in late July 1914, a couple of terrible German policemen arrived in my village with a squad of soldiers in grey-green uniforms. They went to see our policeman, then soon afterwards put up a notice at the town hall with a black, white and red border. It said that war was coming. The villagers knew everything was about to change.

Next, the policemen and soldiers arrested old Father Vetter and searched his house from top to bottom. They couldn't find Yerri Klipfel: he had escaped the previous night down to the train station, hiding in a coal wagon which had taken him to Switzerland, and then to France. Furious, the policemen arrested his grandfather. The sad procession of the two old men under guard went down the main street to the nearby town prison, where hundreds were already locked up.

This was just the start of the suffering in my village. The very next day, they announced the call-up to the army: every able-bodied man, except the German schoolteacher, was to be drafted and sent to Prussia or Russia to fight. Sometimes we heard gunfire in the distance and dared to hope, but then it would fade away and the village returned to silent sadness. Regiments of grey soldiers trooped past with their guns.

Before long, the policeman announced that Germany needed our wheat, our gold, wool from our mattresses, our copper. One day they took the bells from the old church tower, to melt down.

The German schoolteacher, whose name, I can now say, was Stupfel, was terrified of being sent to the trenches, so he turned to policing, spying and reporting people to the authorities, as well enthusiastically telling us about great German victories. He made the children bring copper utensils from their homes. He took children into the forest to collect nettles for making cloth, acorns for extracting oil, and berries for making vast amounts of jam. He showed no shame in using them to find out if their families still hoped for a French victory. No evil deed was beneath him. Even more than the policeman, he was the tyrant of the village.

But everything comes to an end, even the cruellest hardships. One fine day, we saw the grey soldiers pouring back towards the river Rhine, tired and disorganized. An aeroplane with a red, white and blue emblem flew over and dropped papers announcing a French victory. Soon afterwards, a carriage arrived at the policeman's house, and Irmentrude, Hildegarde, Elsa and Hilda got in, with lots of bags. The German schoolteacher got in too, although not before the crowd pulled off his *tricolore* hat ribbon. They all left to the sound of boos and threatening cries, mingled with the children's shouts of joy.

The same day, Father Vetter and grandfather Klipfel returned from exile, tired and thin. A huge wave of joy swept over us. We were French again. We cried and hugged each other in the street, and Father Vetter and the school nun quickly taught the children to sing our national anthem, the *Marseillaise*. Red, white and blue flags appeared at every window and garlands of flowers and paper lanterns were hung from every pretty wooden balcony. Father Schimmel climbed up the church tower to fly his old flag.

A few days later, a fine French regiment arrived. Everyone went out to meet them, and they came into the village laden with flowers, escorted by all the young girls and children of the last village they'd been through. As they entered, Father Vetter, his voice choked with tears, made a speech to the colonel that he must have been preparing for forty-seven years.

We had set up long tables with white tablecloths in the main square, and they were decorated with *Kougelhopf* and *Bretzels*, tarts, aniseed bread and slim bottles of Alsatian white wine. There was also a stage and, while the victorious solders drank their cup of honour, the young girls of the village came in their best traditional dress and sang the *Marseillaise* and a song of freedom for Alsace-Lorraine. It was so beautiful and moving that I cannot find words to describe the moment.

HANSI September 1920

This illustrated book is the master work of an artist at his best. From its first appearance in 1913, *My Village* was widely applauded for the progressive modern style of its artwork. Techniques of light borrowed from impressionism and the Japanese-style engravings of the early twentieth century, prefigured the work of the great book illustrators who followed.

Hansi helps us explore the Alsace of legend, picturesque and proud of its past. He had made a careful study of the villages and traditional dress of the northern part of his native region, and here recreates a rural world of folklore in an area which had become essentially modernized and urban.

The work of a militant, *My Village* depicts the issue of Alsace's political protest against the domination of Germany which, in 1871, annexed a bordering province which for two centuries had been French. In opposition to this period of French influence, Germany stressed its own linguistic and historic claims based on eight centuries of Alsace's absorption into the German-dominated Holy Roman Empire. Hansi's often uncompromising text expresses the desire of committed Alsatians for more autonomy from Germany.

The work was banned in Germany from the time of its first printing in France, and its author prosecuted by German courts. Hansi's trial, in July 1914, contributed to the rising tension in Europe as the First World War loomed on the horizon. Found guilty of incitement to violent resistance, Hansi fled to France and enlisted some weeks later in the French army. *My Village* became a propaganda weapon of the Allies and its fame rapidly spread.

The book's widespread success continues to this day, and Hansi's work still presents a delightful picture of Alsace which is full of nostalgia and charm.

Benoît Bruant, biographer of Hansi
Hansi. L'artiste tendre et rebelle, La Nuée Bleue, 2008

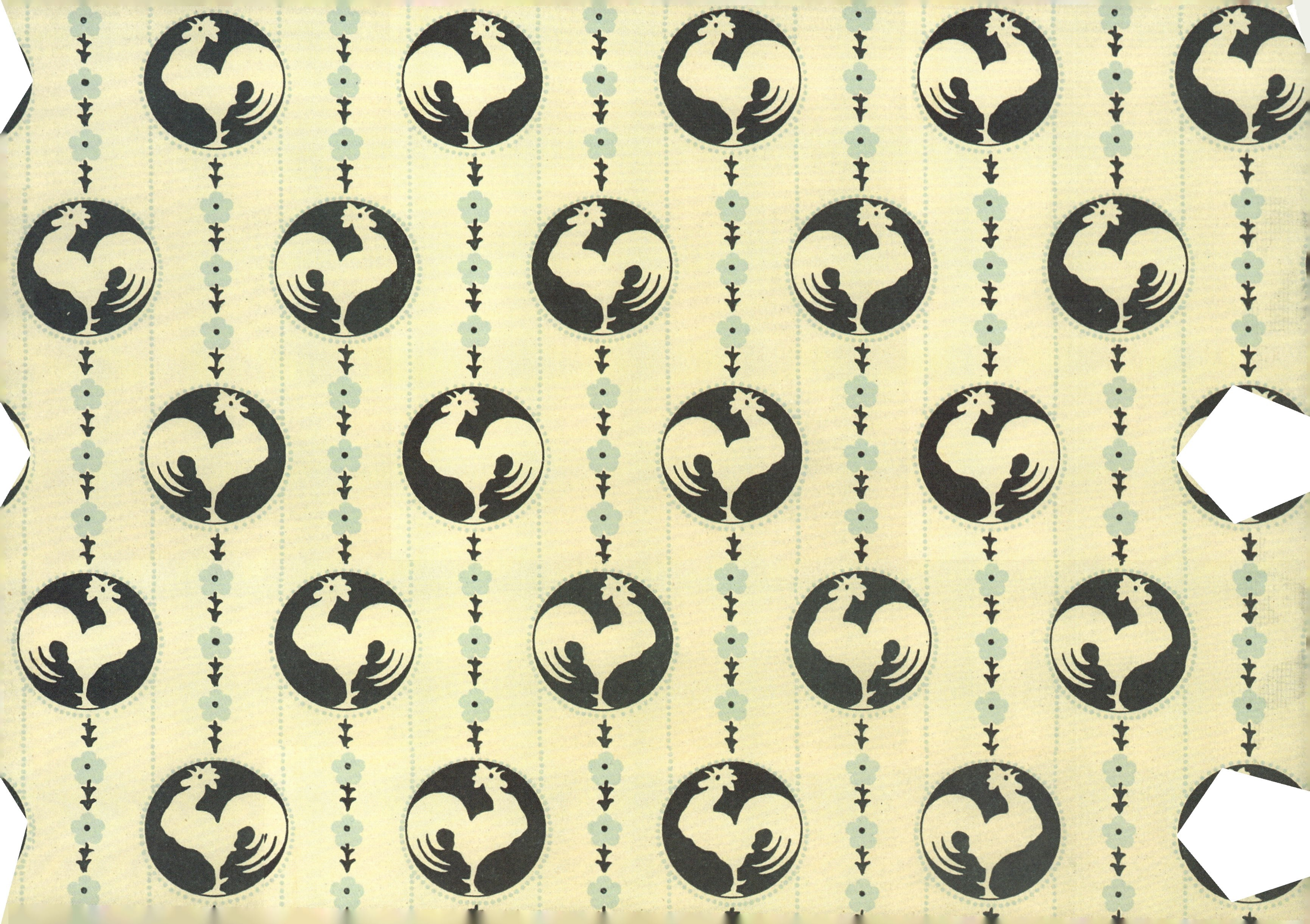